Under the Sea
DOT-TO-DOT

Evan & Lael Kimble

Illustrated by Richard Salvucci

Sterling Publishing Co., Inc.
New York

10 9 8

Published by Sterling Publishing Company, Inc.
387 Park Avenue South, New York, N.Y. 10016
© 1997 by Evan and Lael Kimble
Distributed in Canada by Sterling Publishing
% Canadian Manda Group, One Atlantic Avenue, Suite 105
Toronto, Ontario, Canada M6K 3E7
Distributed in Great Britain by Chris Lloyd at Orca Book Servies,
Stanley House, Fleets Lane, Poole BH15 3AJ England
Distributed in Australia by Capricorn Link (Australia) Pty, Ltd.
P.O. Box 704, Windsor, NSW 2756 Australia
Printed in China
All rights reserved

Sterling ISBN 0-8069-6152-X

Contents

Angelfish

Size:	3 to 24 inches (7.5 to 60cm)
Color:	Usually silvery, with dark markings, but it may be a solid blue, yellow, gold, or part black.
What it eats:	Sponges, algae, and plants
Where it lives:	In shallow waters in coral reefs and lagoons, but some types like deep water.

Angelfish are some of the most beautiful and color-ful fish of all. Many scientists think that their bright colors help confuse their enemies and keep them away. The colors also help them attract mates.

Some angelfish live as some human families do. Many of the males and females travel in pairs, stay mated for life, and take care of their eggs and their young. They swim and eat during the day and sleep in holes at night. Sometimes, angelfish sleep in the same hole night after night, the same way humans go back to the same bed!

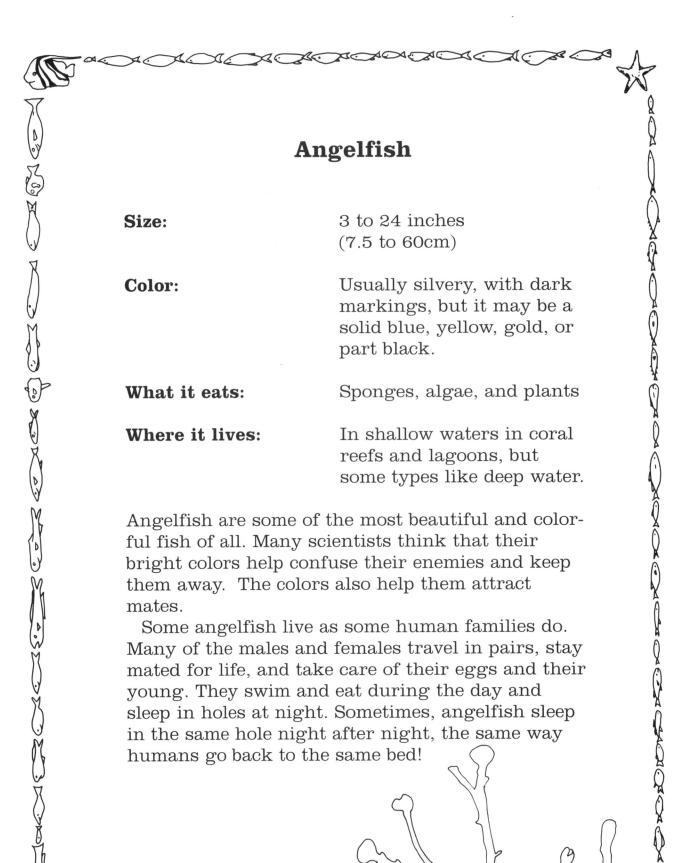

Algae are small creatures that look like plants and live in water.

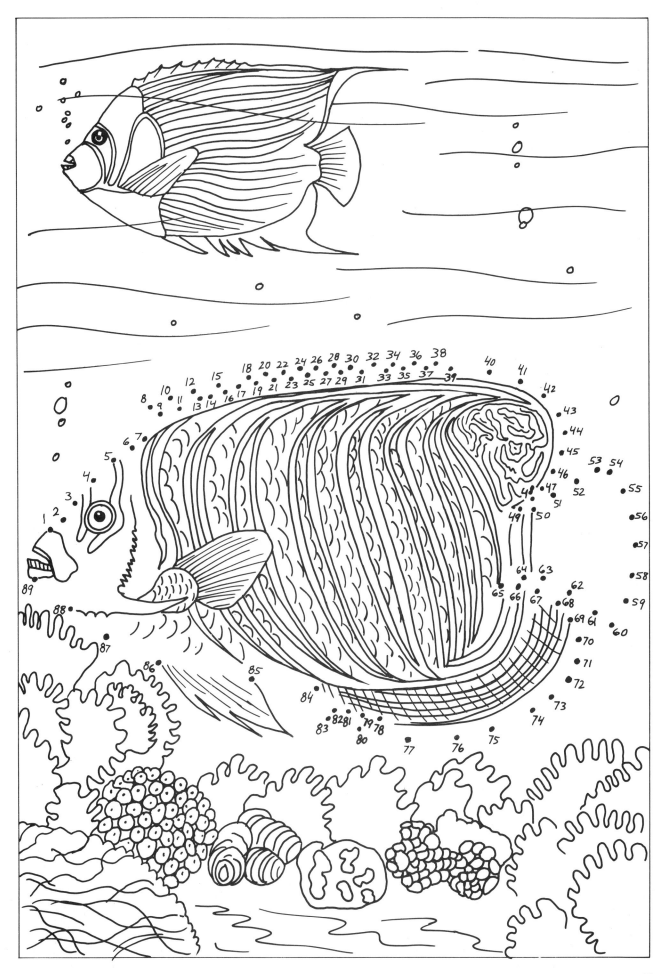

Angler
(also called the Lurefish or Monkfish)

Size: Up to 4 feet (1.2m) long, but most are much smaller

Color: Black with red markings, but most are drab colors that blend with the ocean floor

What it eats: Fish, crustaceans, and jellyfish—sometimes larger than itself!

Where it lives: At the sea bottom

Anglers are named for the way they fish for their prey. Females (and, in some types, males) have a long fishing-rod kind of arm, with a fleshy bait at the tip. The arm ranges from short to long, and the bait is often red and shaped like a worm. Sometimes it glows! Many fish are attracted to this lure and get close enough for the angler to swallow them.

Crustaceans, like lobsters, crabs, and shrimp (shown here), live inside a hard shell.

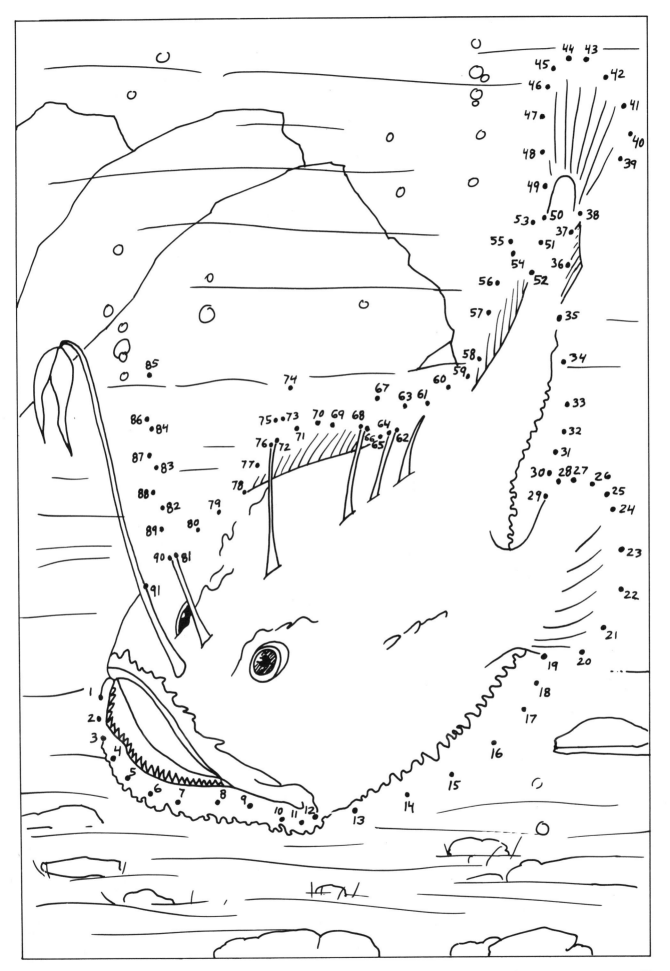

Barnacle

Size:	Usually, a quarter of an inch (.6cm) to 5 inches (12.5cm) across—sometimes as big as 30 inches (75cm)
Color:	White or gray
What it eats:	Small drifting plants and plankton (see page 12)
Where it lives:	In almost all waters, warm and cold, deep and shallow

Barnacles look like a kind of shell, but when they're alive, there is a creature inside that looks like a shrimp. When you see something coming out of the top of a barnacle, it's the feet of the creature trying to kick food into its mouth. Its head is deep inside.

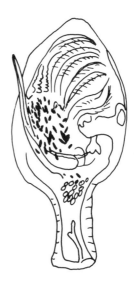

The insides of a barnacle

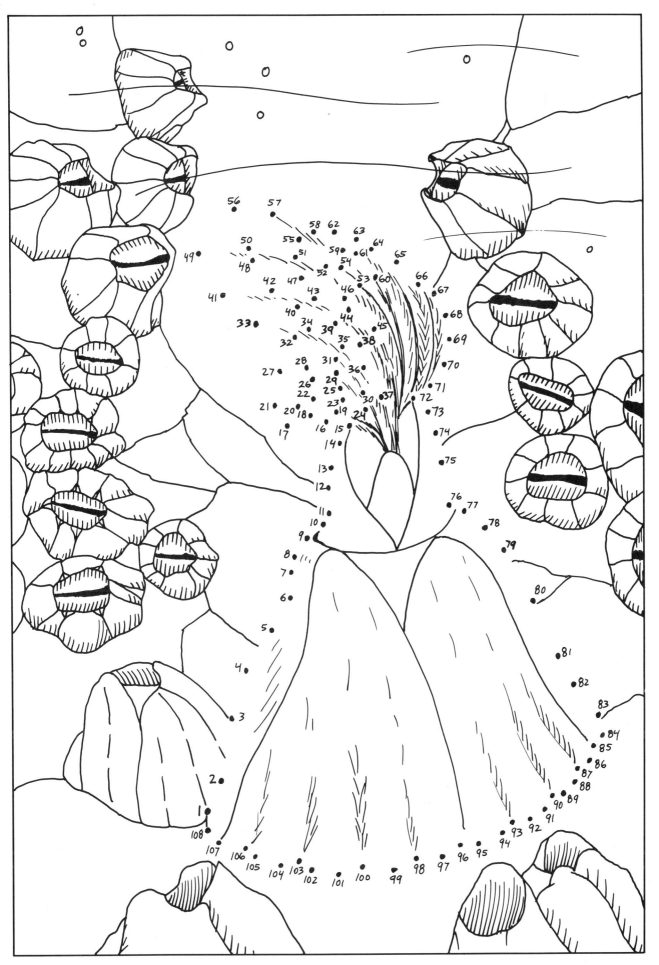

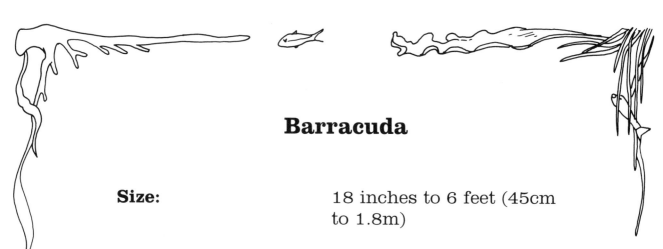

Barracuda

Size: 18 inches to 6 feet (45cm to 1.8m)

Color: Silver with dark spots below and gray to green along the top of the back. Some types are blue to brown along the back.

What it eats: Fish, especially smaller ones, like mullets, anchovies, and grunts, shrimps and squids.

Where it lives: In ocean waters of tropical regions and some temperate areas

Barracudas have a big mouth full of long teeth that look like dogs' teeth, only the barracuda's are sharp as a razor. Their bodies are usually silver and shiny, but they change color to match the reef in which they hide as they wait to jump out and capture small fish. They can swim very fast—up to 22 miles an hour.

Barracudas are curious fish. They like to swim with scuba divers, and most types won't bite a human unless someone scares it.

Grunts are fish that got their name from the sounds they make when they grind their teeth.

Blue Whale

Size: As long as 100 feet (30m)
                    and as heavy as 150 tons

Color: Mottled blue-gray

What it eats: Crustaceans and plankton

Where it lives: In warm and cold ocean
                    waters

The blue whale is the largest of all known animals,
even including most dinosaurs! Seven cars could
line up on the back of a large one, and it can weigh
as much as a town of 2,000 people. In the first six
months of its life, it gains 10 pounds an hour!

   The blue whale is found alone or in small groups
in all oceans. It spends the summer in polar waters
and in the winter it moves toward the Equator to
breed.

The Blue Whale
does not hunt for
its food. Like most
really large whales,
it doesn't even have
teeth. It just swims
along, taking in
water that is filled
with plankton
(pictured here)—
tiny animals and
plants that are its
main food.

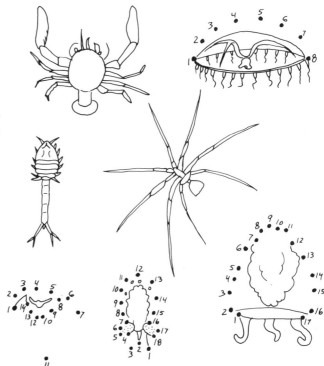

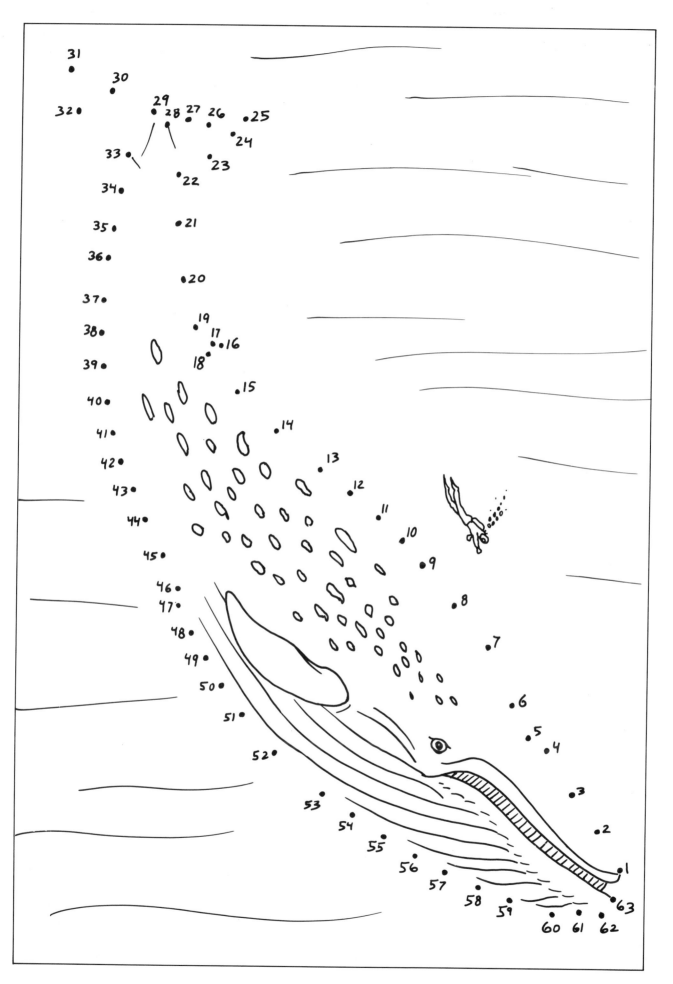

31
30
32 29 28 27 26 25
33 24
34 23
22
35 21
36
20
37
38 19 17 16
39 18
15
40
41 14
42 13
43 12
44 11
45 10
46 9
47
48 8
49 7
50
51 6
5
52 4
53 3
54 2
55
56 1
57
58 63
59
60 61 62

13

Coral

Size:

A single coral may be .2 to 2 inches (5 to 50mm). A reef of corals usually grows up to 3 feet (1m) high, and one in the Pacific is a mile high!

Color:

The skeletons are white, but the tiny creatures can be pink, red, purple, yellow, green, and golden brown.

What it eats:

Plankton, small shrimp, and tiny fish

Where it lives:

In shallow reefs in warm ocean waters, up to 3 miles (4800m) deep. Some types like cold water.

Corals look just like rock, but they are actually living animals. What you see when you look at them is the skeleton the creature made. The creature lives on top of the stone skeletons of previous generations, and these layers of limestone make up the tropical reefs of the world.

Each coral head is called a polyp (pronounced PAH-lip). It has a mouth and a ring of small arms or tentacles.

This is what it looks like on the inside.

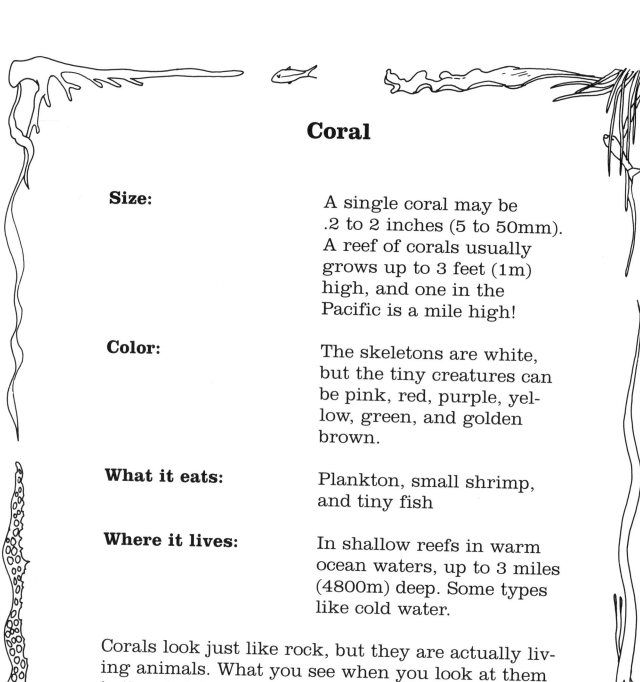

15

Crab

Size:	As small as 1 inch (2.5cm) or as wide as 4 feet (1.2m) across
Color:	Tan, brown, red, green, blue-gray
What it eats:	Mostly snails, clams, and other small fish
Where it lives:	On the sea floor

Crabs are almost completely covered by a hard shell. Their bodies are flattened, and they have five pairs of legs. They use eight of their legs to walk on, and the two in front are shaped like claws.

The eyes of crabs are on stalks. When a crab is in danger, it retreats inside its shell and then slowly creeps out, eyes first, to see if it's safe.

The hermit crab is a special kind of crab that wears old shells of snails and other creatures. It must find larger shells to live in as it grows up.

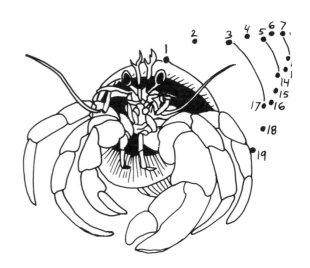

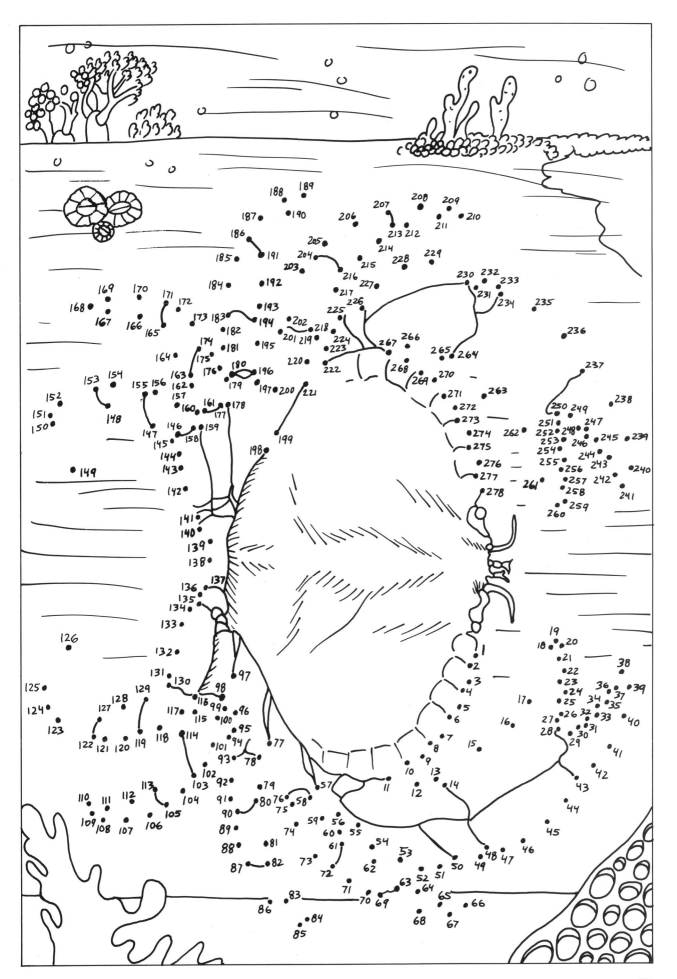

Dolphin

Size: 3 to 13 feet (1 to 3.9m) long

Color: Gray, blackish, or brown

What it eats: Fish, squids, shrimps

Where it lives: In warm and temperate seas

Dolphins are small, streamlined whales. They are graceful, smart, and playful—and friendly to humans. They usually live in large groups, and "talk" to each other through a range of sounds and ultrasonic pulses.

Like other whales, they find objects in the water by using sound. They send out clicking sounds that bounce off objects and send back an echo, which tells the dolphins where the objects are.

Most dolphins are protective of one another. If one of them is in trouble, it sends a distress call and others come to help.

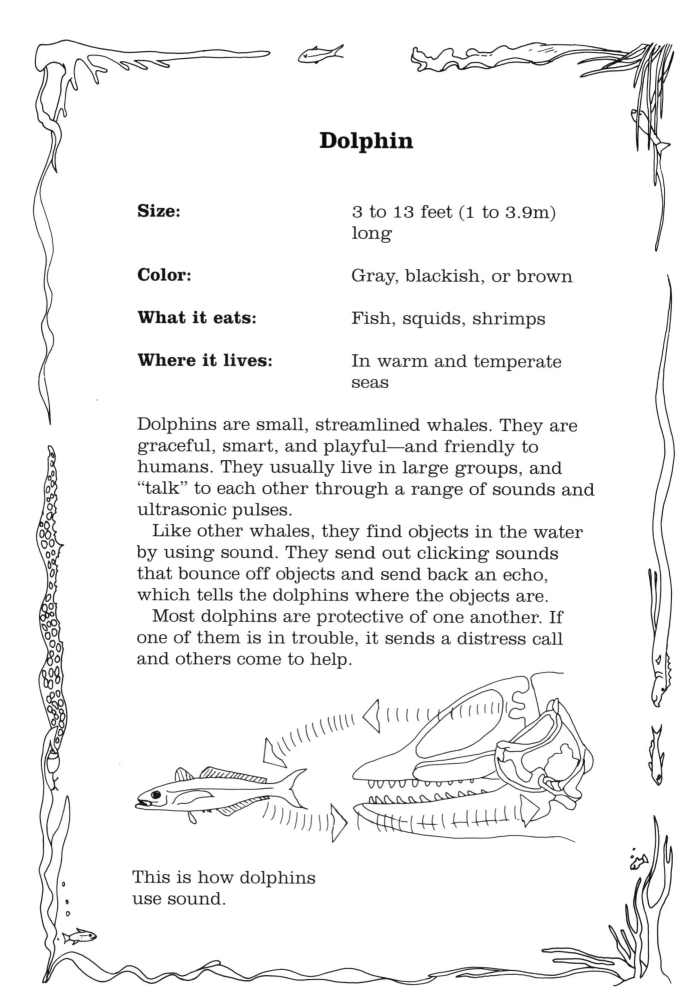

This is how dolphins use sound.

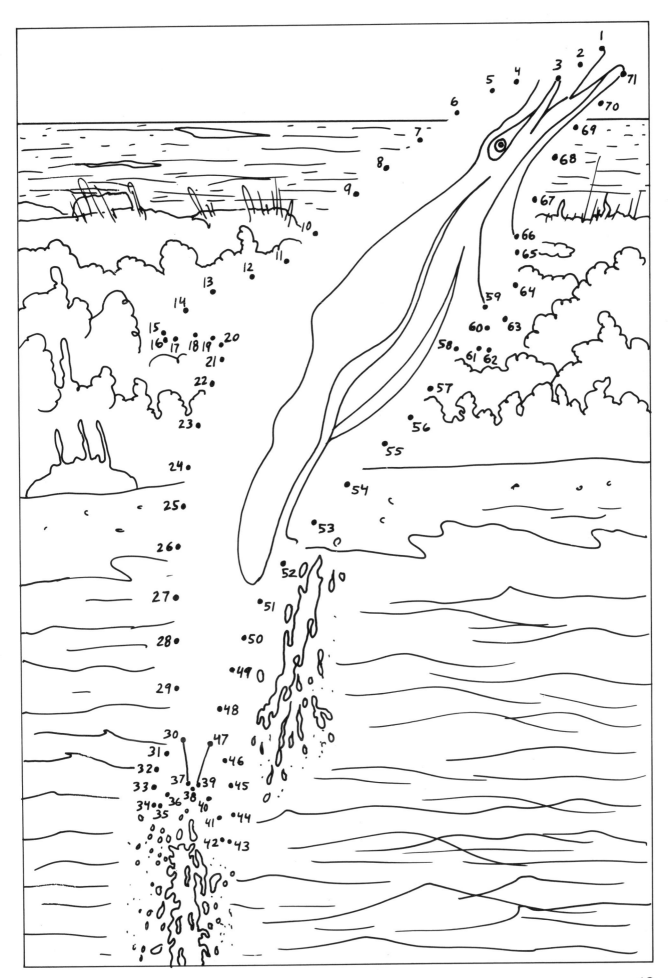

Electric Eel

Size: About 9 feet (2.7m) long
                        and weighing up to 49
                        pounds (22kg)

Color: Gray-brown

What it eats: Mostly fish

Where it lives: In freshwater streams in
                        South America

An electric eel is capable of giving an electric
shock strong enough to stun a human being. The
electric organs are in its tail, and the shock comes
from the creature's muscles and nerves. The shock
is used mainly to stun and capture fish and other
prey. The eel can use this power whenever it
wants. The jolt can measure up to 650 volts.

650 volts is more than five
times the power in a 60 watt
light bulb!

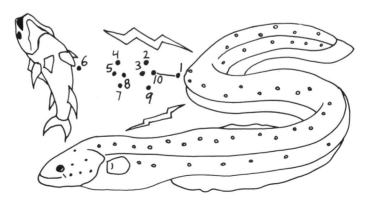

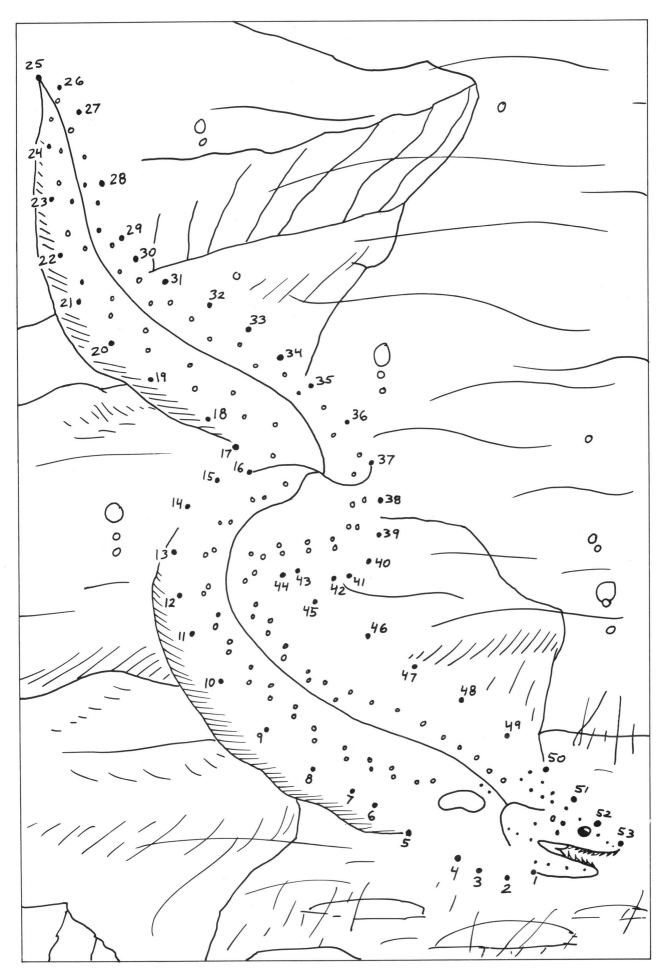

Great White Shark

Size: About 18 feet (5.4m) and weighing up to a ton and a half

Color: Dark gray above, white below

What it eats: Seals, sea lions, fish, other sharks, and rays

Where it lives: In the open seas

The shark is an ancient fish. It is so well suited for life in the sea that it has remained the same for the last 300 million years.

A fearsome hunter, it is fast and has long, sharp teeth with jagged edges, good for tearing its prey. These teeth are sometimes as long as two inches (5cm).

The jaws of a Great White Shark can crush a small boat.

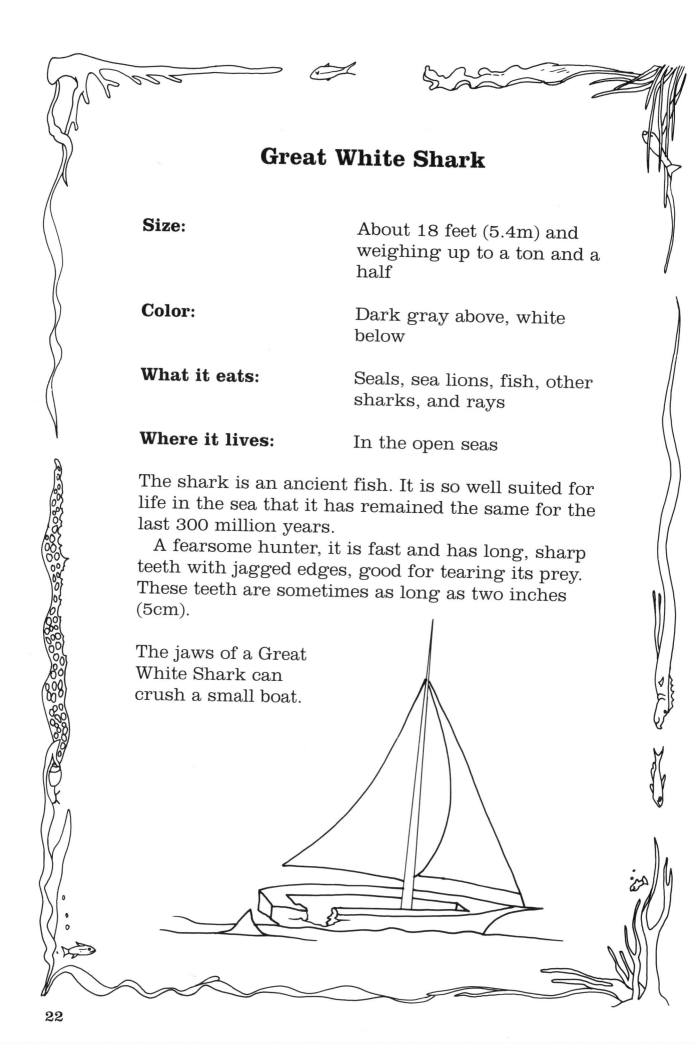

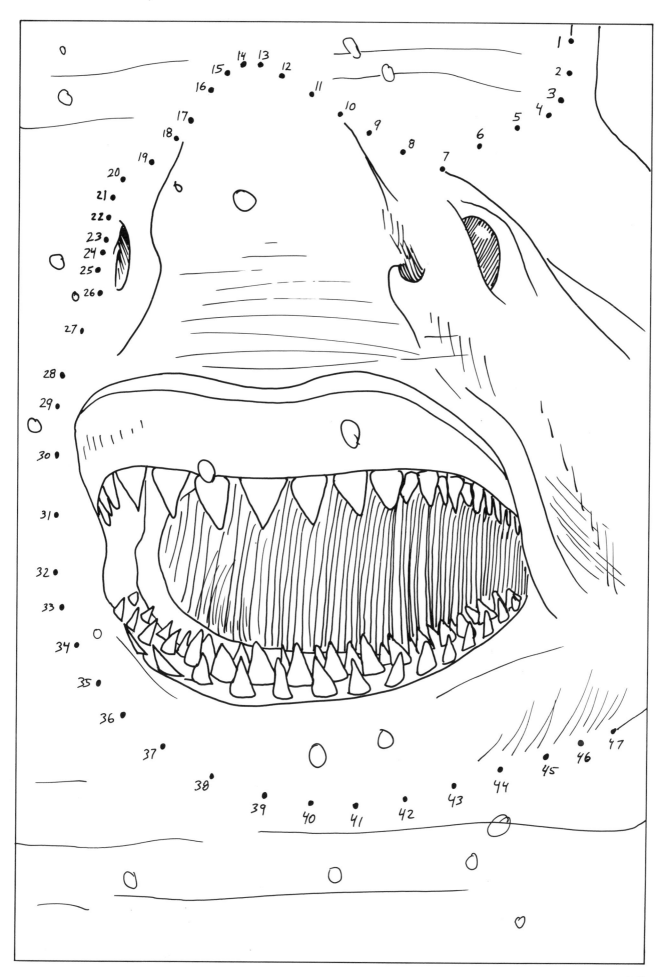

Kissing Fish
(also called Gourami)

Size: Usually about 10 inches (25cm) long

Color: White, silvery green, pinkish white

What it eats: Insects, plants, algae

Where it lives: In tropical freshwater

Many fish fight over where they lay their eggs and over who will be their mates. Among these fish are "kissing fish," who got their name because they are often seen with their mouths pressed together. But don't think they're really kissing. They are actually battling with each other to see who will win. This fighting is done by both males and females.

When the gourami aren't fighting among themselves, they are trying to keep away from bigger fish, such as this catfish, who likes to eat them.

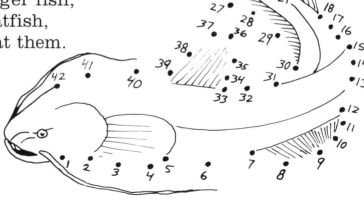

Lionfish

Size: Usually about 16 inches (40 cm), but they can be up to 39 inches long.

Color: Red, white, pink, or brown, some with striped zebra-like markings

What it eats: Small fish and shellfish

Where it lives: In coral reefs in tropical waters in the Pacific and Indian oceans, the Red Sea, and the Persian Gulf

The lionfish has long, flowing fins and beautiful colors—but don't touch! Its spines are sharp and poisonous and touching them can cause intense pain. People have even died from touching them.

    Most of the time, the lionfish swims along slowly, but once it spots its prey, it darts forward and strikes with lightning speed.

Can you tell how the lionfish got its name

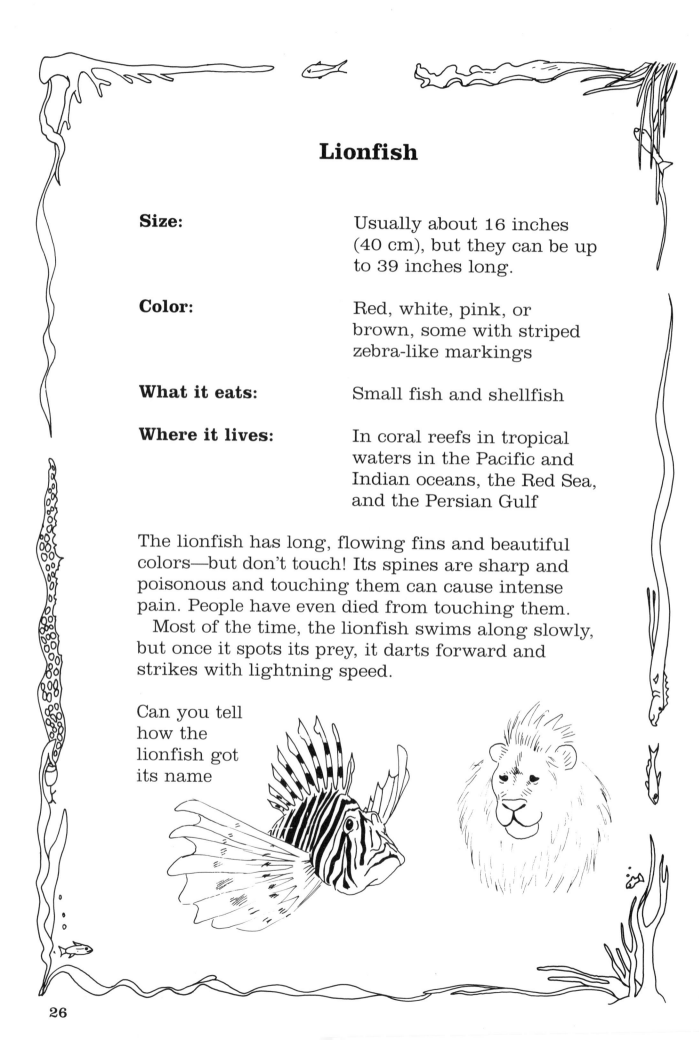

Lobster

Size: Usually about 12 to 18 inches (30 to 45cm), not including its antennae (feelers)

Color: Grayish orange

What it eats: Snails, worms, mollusks, shrimp

Where it lives: In reefs, caves, holes, and under ledges in summer, and in deep water during the winter

Lobsters hunt by night and hide during the day. They have good eyesight and a very strong sense of touch. Their long antennae (feelers) and stiff body hairs make them able to sense the slightest movement around them.

Lobsters shed their hard shell-like covering as they get larger. They grow a new shell underneath, which is soft at first. Lobsters are in danger from predators until the new shell hardens.

Mollusks are animals with shells—like clams (shown here), oysters, and mussels—and also octopuses and squids.

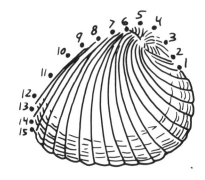

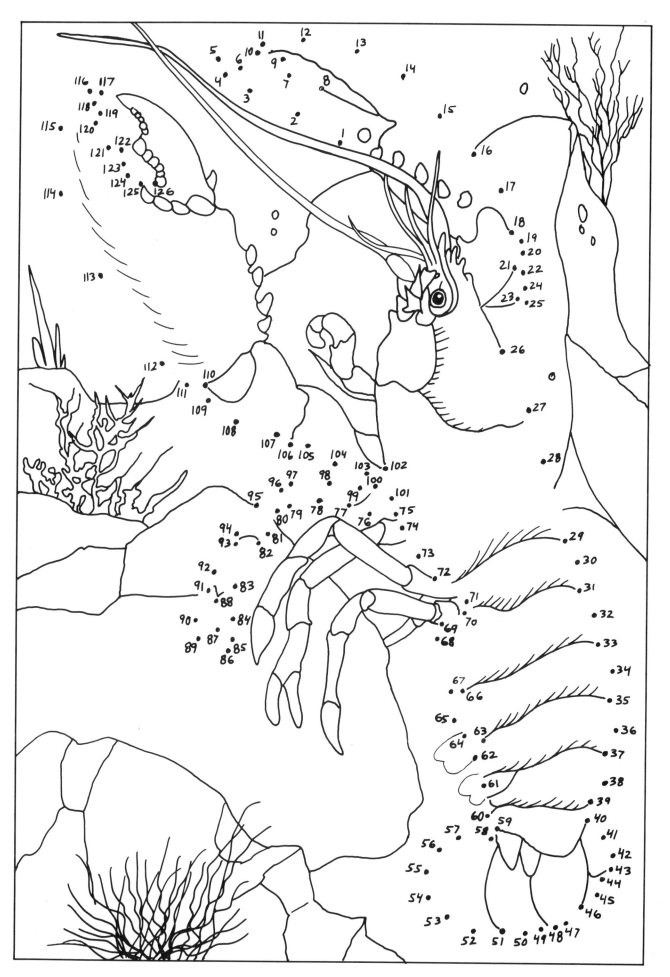

Manatee

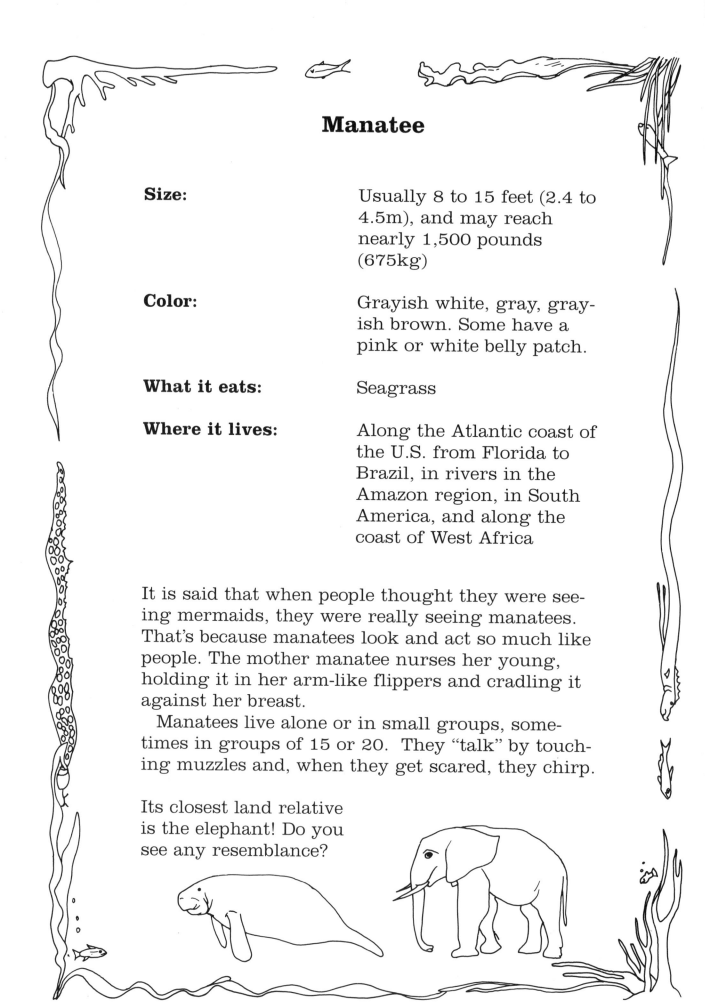

Size: Usually 8 to 15 feet (2.4 to 4.5m), and may reach nearly 1,500 pounds (675kg)

Color: Grayish white, gray, grayish brown. Some have a pink or white belly patch.

What it eats: Seagrass

Where it lives: Along the Atlantic coast of the U.S. from Florida to Brazil, in rivers in the Amazon region, in South America, and along the coast of West Africa

It is said that when people thought they were seeing mermaids, they were really seeing manatees. That's because manatees look and act so much like people. The mother manatee nurses her young, holding it in her arm-like flippers and cradling it against her breast.

Manatees live alone or in small groups, sometimes in groups of 15 or 20. They "talk" by touching muzzles and, when they get scared, they chirp.

Its closest land relative is the elephant! Do you see any resemblance?

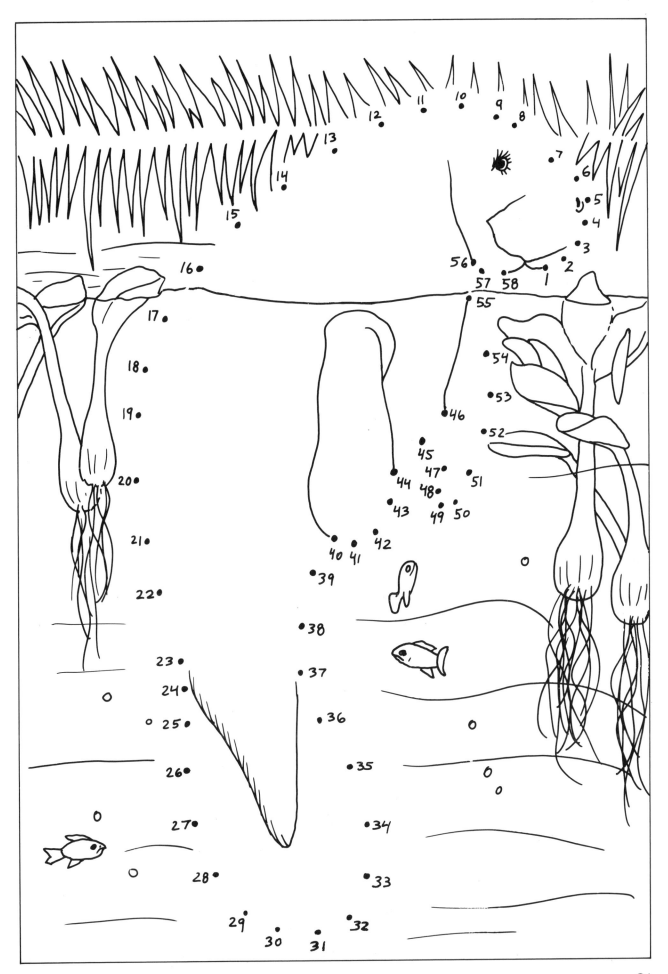

Manta Ray

Size: 3 to 22 feet (.9 to 6.6m) across, depending on the type. The largest one, the Atlantic Manta, weighs in at over two tons!

Color: Reddish to olive-brown, or black on top with gray and black splotches underneath

What it eats: Plankton, fish, shellfish, worms, and other small animals

Where it lives: In oceans all over the world, in the middle and bottom depths

Rays are the graceful cousins of sharks. Both have bodies made of a soft substance called cartilage—like what the tip of your nose is made of.

The fins of manta rays work like the wings of a bird. With them, rays can glide through the water very quickly. They simply flap their underwater wings. But mantas can't swim backwards. Think about it: Have you ever seen a bird fly backwards?

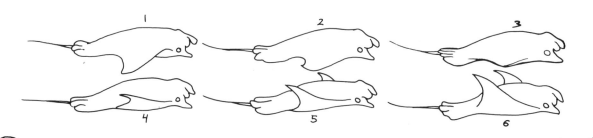

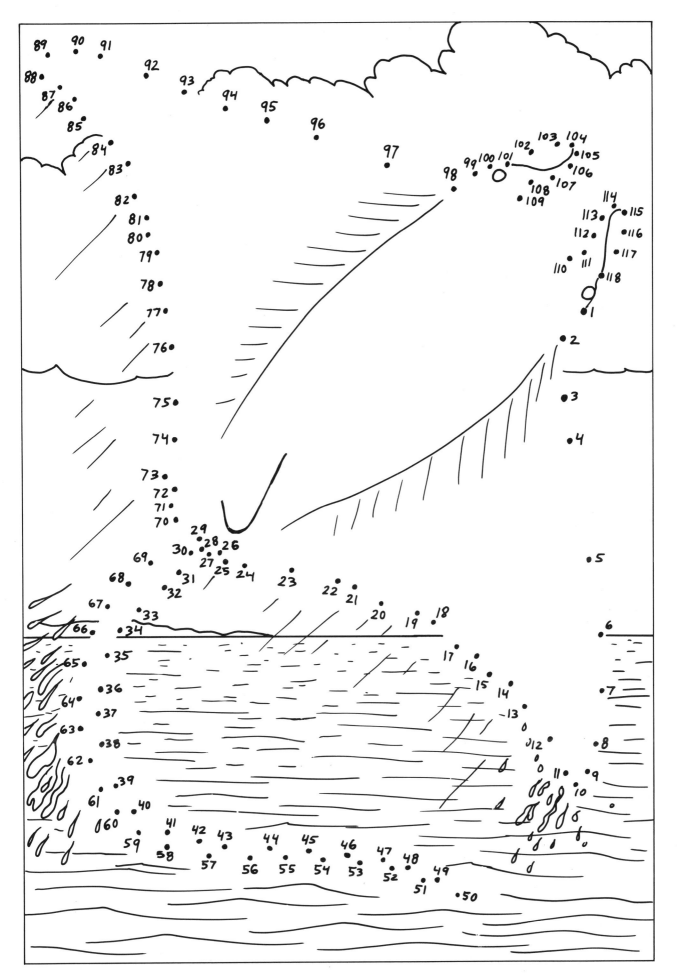

Narwhal

Size:

Usually about 15 feet (4.5m) long. Males have a tusk that is sometimes as long as 9 feet (2.7m).

Color:

Dark bluish gray or brownish. Adults have spots on their backs and sides.

What it eats:

Shrimp, squid, cuttlefish, halibut, cod, and other cold-water fish

Where it lives:

In the Arctic, in very cold waters

A type of whale, the narwhal is often called "the seagoing unicorn," because the male has a single horn that grows out of its head. This horn is actually a great big tooth that twists as it grows. Although it doesn't help the narwhal to chew, it does help it break up ice in polar waters.

The cuttlefish is from the same family as the octopus and squid. It has ten arms and produces an ink called sepia.

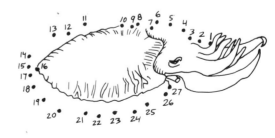

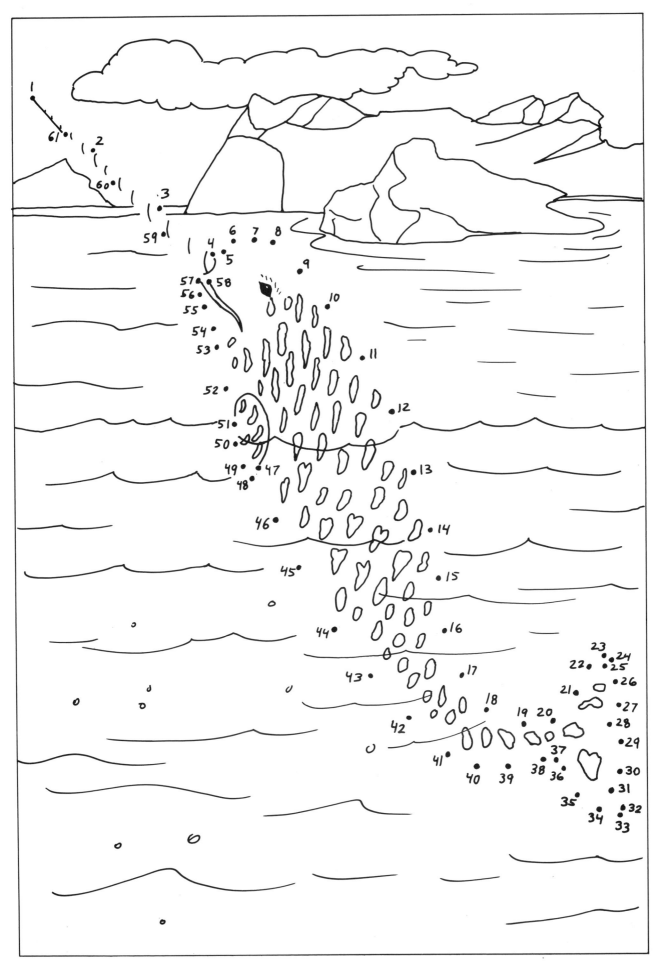

Nautilus

Size:	Usually 10 to 16 inches (25 to 40cm) across
Color:	Brown and white
What it eats:	Shrimp and fish
Where it lives:	Worldwide in fresh and salt water. Some live at the surface, and some on the sea bottom

The Nautilus is a creature that lives inside a shell that it makes by itself. Inside the shell are 36 chambers, and the nautilus lives in the one nearest the outside. The other chambers hold air and water which help the nautilus float.

One of the most amazing things about the nautilus is that its closest relatives are the octopus and the squid!

This is what the nautilus looks like inside its shell.

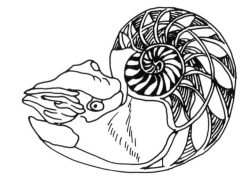

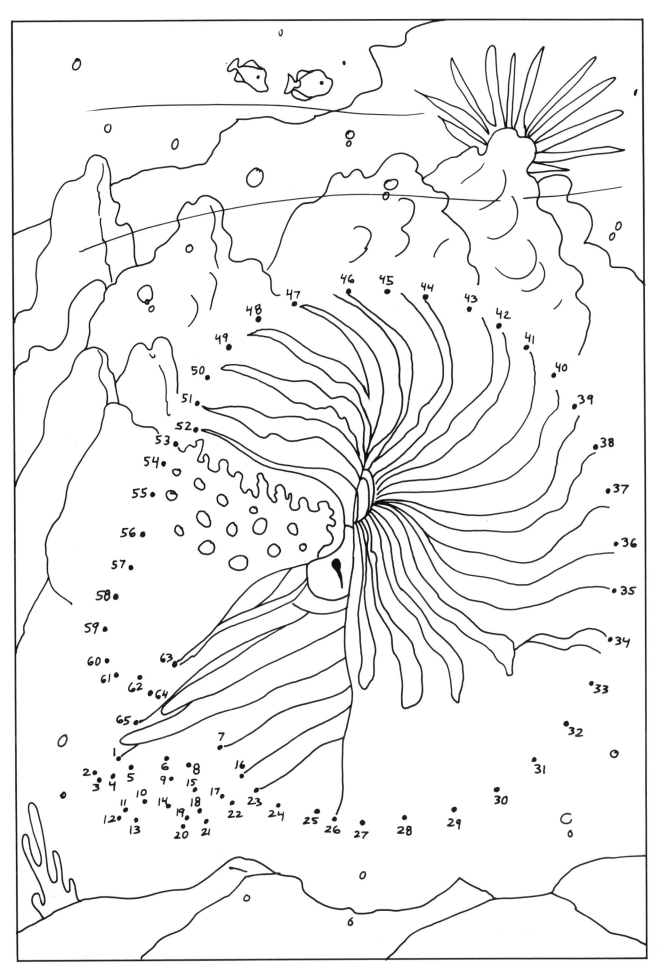

Octopus

Size:	From about 2 inches (5cm) to 18 feet (5.4m) long, with an arm span of almost 30 feet (9m)!
Color:	Most are off-white, but they also may be anything from blue-green to reddish orange
What it eats:	Mostly worms, fish, crustaceans, and other mollusks. Some eat plankton.
Where it lives:	At the bottom of the sea in tropical and temperate waters

Neither octopuses nor squids have tough skin or a shell to protect them. Instead, octopuses hide by changing color. If they are caught, they shoot out an inky fog to keep their enemy from finding them.

The octopus has eight arms (or tentacles) that help it to catch its prey. Some types also squirt poison from their mouth that makes their prey unable to move so they can eat it.

The octopus is often a meal of the moray eel, called "the rattlesnake of the deep" because it strikes like a snake, poisoning its prey.

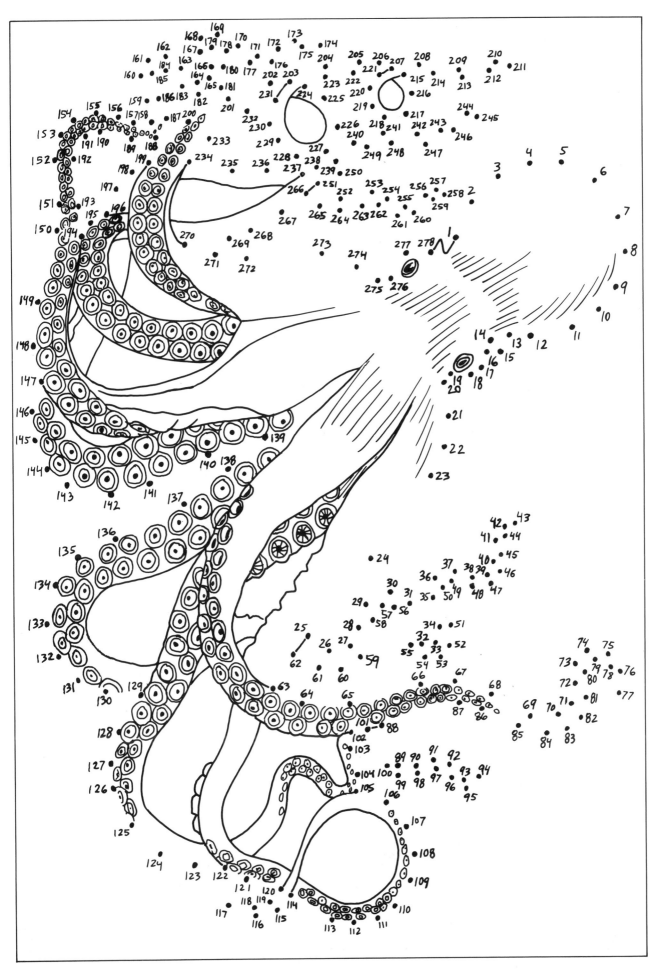

Orca
(also known as the Killer Whale)

Size:

As long as 31 feet (9.3m) and weighing as much as 11,000 pounds (over 5 tons). The fin on its back can grow as tall as 6 feet (1.8m).

Color:

Usually black with white on the underparts, above each eye, and on each flank

What it eats:

Fish, penguins, squid, octopus, seals, dolphins, and other whales

Where it lives:

In coastal seas in the Arctic and the Antarctic—sometimes also in tropical seas

Though they're called "killer whales," these creatures don't hurt people. They are dolphins, powerful hunters, and they swim in formation, either in a line or in rows, hunting in packs.

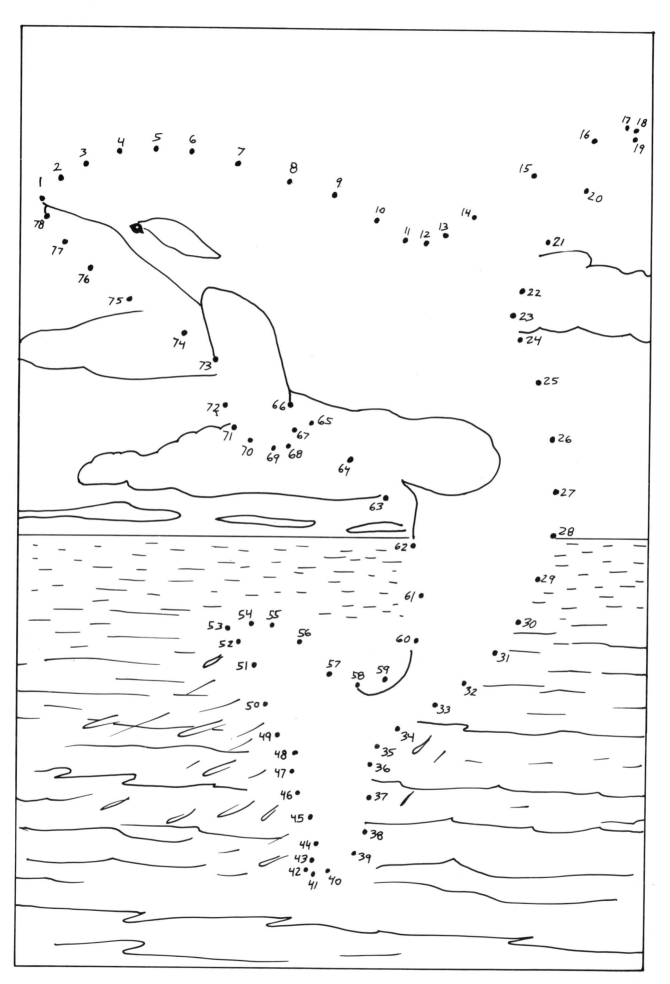

Portuguese Man-of-War

Size: 3 to 12 inches (7.50 to 30cm) across, but its tentacles can grow up to 165 feet (50m)!

Color: Transparent and tinted with pink, blue, or violet

What it eats: Plankton and small fish

Where it lives: In warm seas all over the world

The man-of-war is a huge jellyfish. It has a simple body—just a stomach and a mouth—plus tentacles. It can't chase its prey or swim away from its enemies. Still, the man-of-war is among the most deadly creatures of the sea.

It stings its prey, paralyzing its victims so that it can eat them. Its tentacles contain poison that shoots out if it senses something nearby. Sometimes, even the pressure of a wave will make the poison come out.

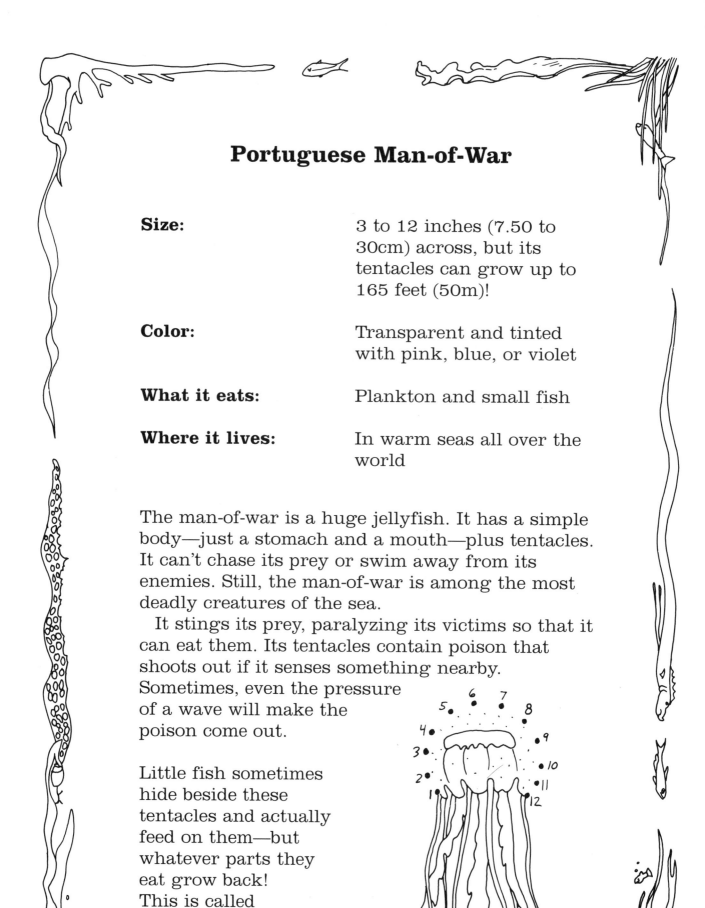

Little fish sometimes hide beside these tentacles and actually feed on them—but whatever parts they eat grow back! This is called "regeneration."

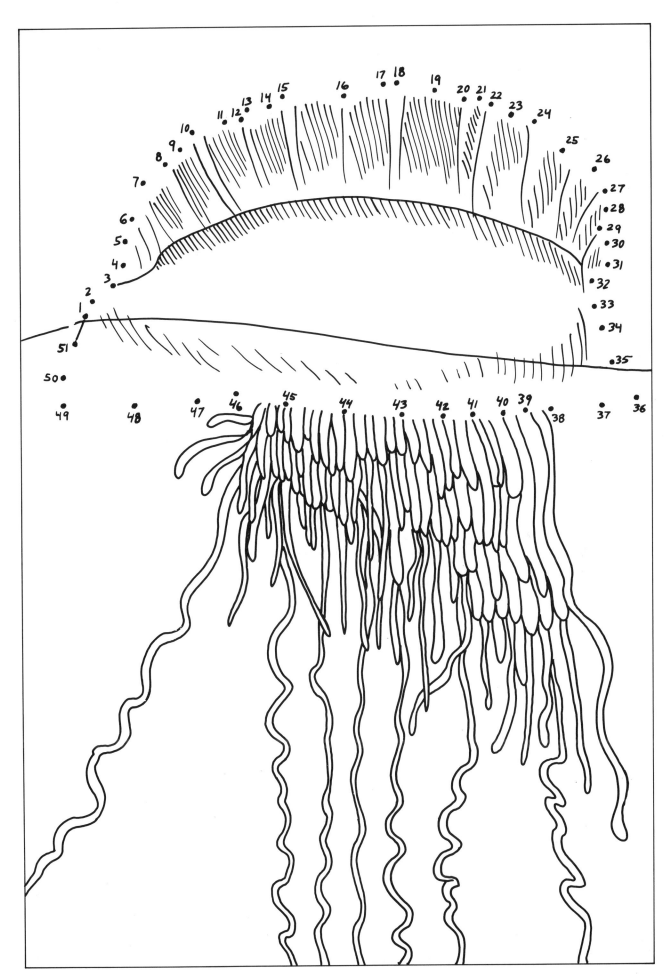

Puffer
(also called Pufferfish, Blowfish, or Swellfish)

Size: The largest grow to be 3 feet (.9m) long.

Color: Yellow with black spots and a white underbelly. Also gray, greenish, blue-green, blue-gray, orange, brown, purple. Most are drab, with markings on their sides and belly.

What it eats: Fish

Where it lives: In warm and temperate waters around the world

Puffers can make themselves really big in order to scare off their enemies. They actually swallow water or take in air to do it, growing to two or three times their normal size. That way, they become too big for their enemies to eat.

Like the puffer, the surgeonfish has added protection—a sharp, bony blade on each side of its body that can cut anyone who tries to attack it.

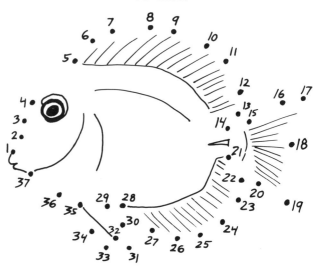

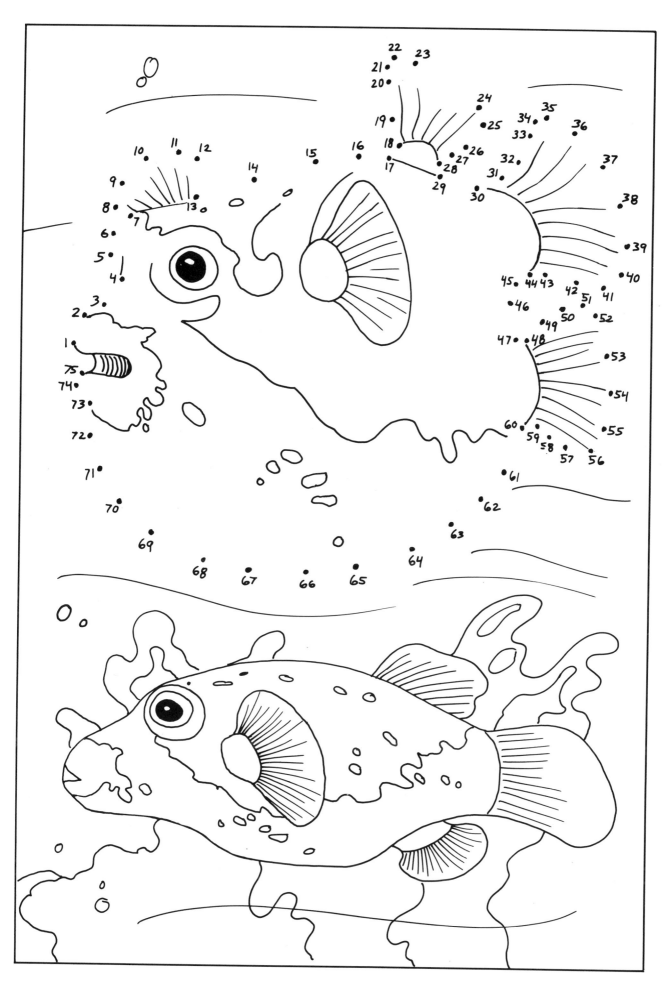

Sea Anemone

Size:	From less than an inch to 5 feet (1.5m) across
Color:	Often yellow, green, blue; sometimes orange, pink, or white. The Orange Ball Anemone (shown here), is white with orange balls attached.
What it eats:	Some eat only tiny plants or animals; others eat larger ones and fish.
Where it lives:	In oceans worldwide

Sea anemones look like plants but they are animals. They are in the same family as the jellyfish (page 42) and coral (page 14). Like the jellyfish, they have poisonous tentacles (arms) that help them catch their food.

The anemone will attach itself to a rock or a plant, but it can detach itself quickly if it senses danger. Then, it creeps along very slowly.

Hermit crabs are often found with sea anemones. The anemone attaches itself to the crab's shell and goes wherever the crab goes. When the crab moves to a new shell, so does the anemone.

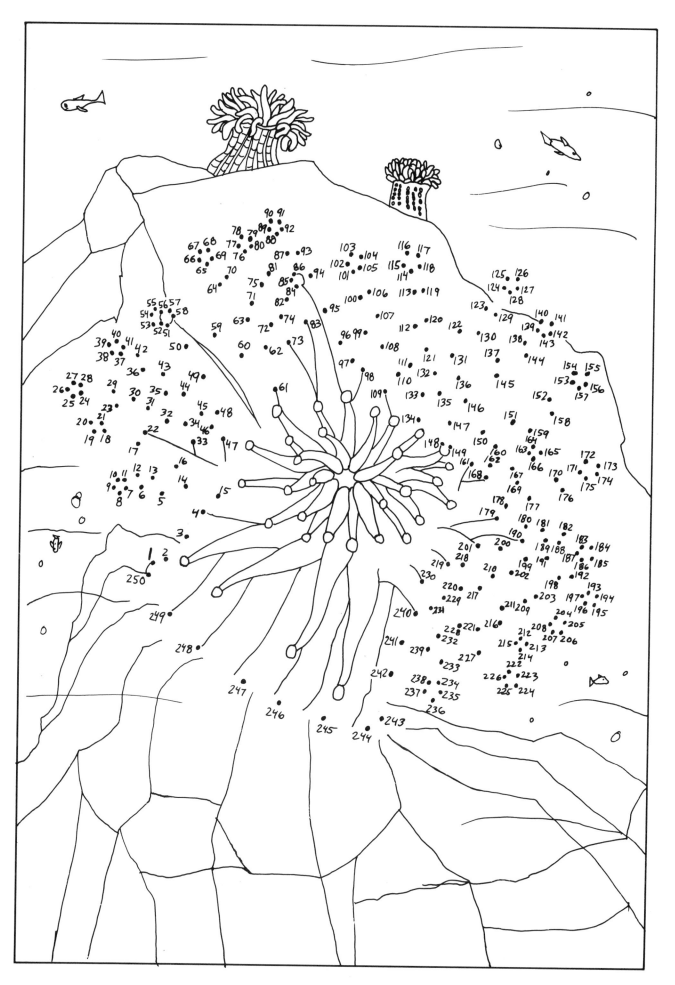

Sea Horse

Size: Most are 3 to 5 inches (7.5 to 12.5cm) long.

Color: Orange, red, and white, but mostly brown

What it eats: Plankton

Where it lives: In coral reefs and shallow waters off the Atlantic coasts of England, Africa, North America, and also the Pacific coast of North America.

An amazing fact about sea horses is that the father has the babies. The female lays eggs in a pouch in the belly of the male. Six weeks later, the babies hatch. The father grasps a seaweed stem with his tail and bends backwards and forward to stretch his pouch. As the pouch widens, the baby sea horses shoot out. The babies are born in batches of five or so, and the birth can last two full days.

Can you tell why this creature is called a Sea Horse?

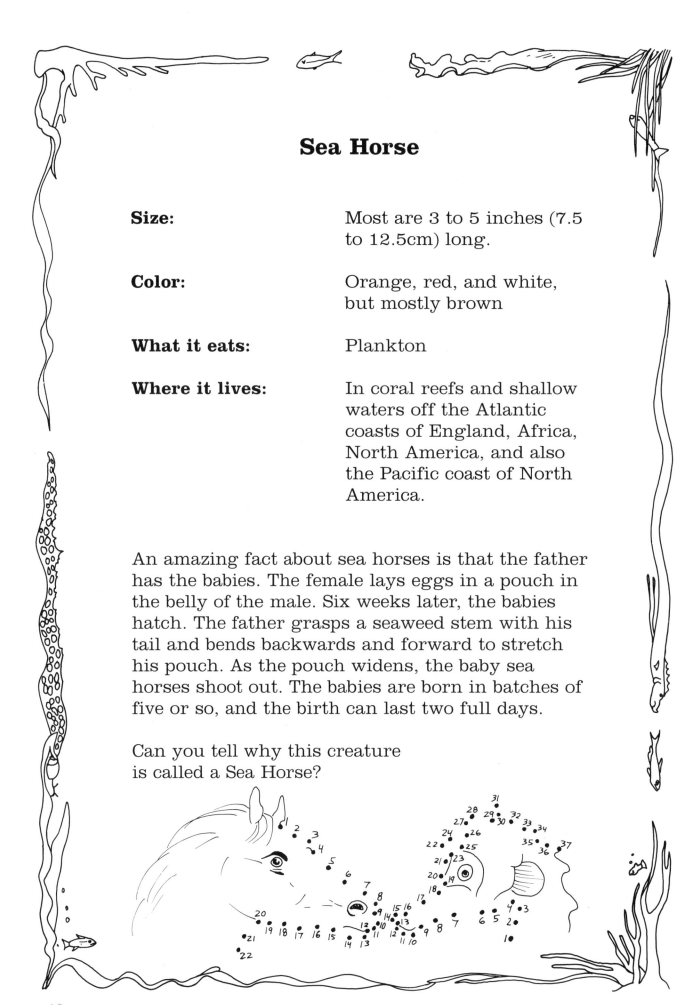

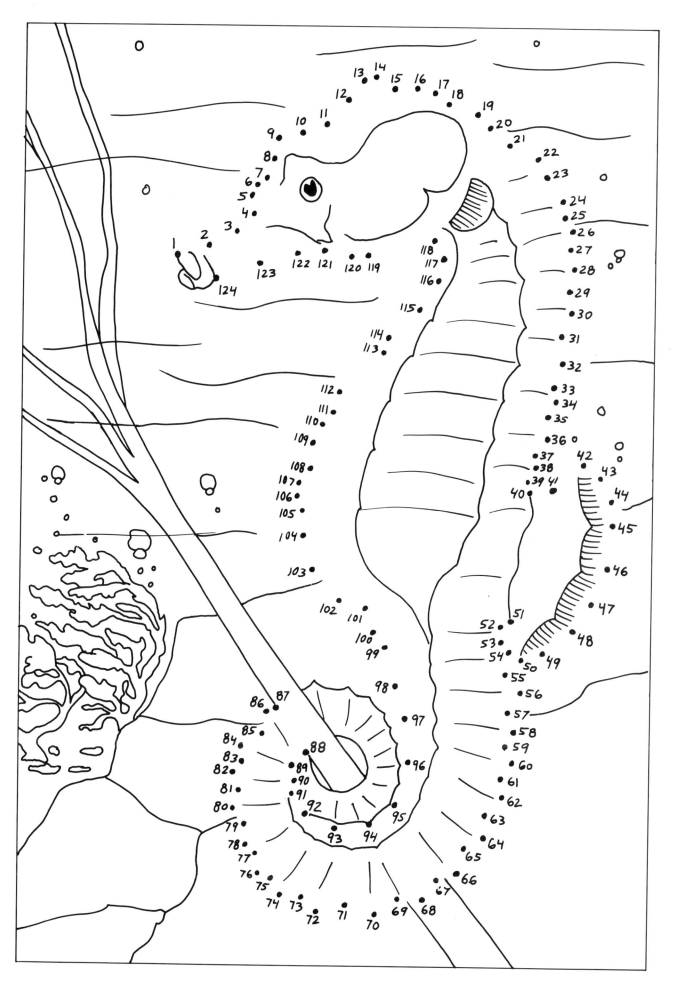

Seal

Size: Ranging from about 3 feet (.9m) long and weighing about 150 pounds (67.5kg) to—in the case of the elephant seal—21 feet (6.3m) long and 7,780 pounds (3501kg).

Color: Gray or brown

What it eats: Mainly fish and sometimes squid, other mollusks, and penguins

Where it lives: Throughout the world— some in the open ocean and others in coastal waters, spending time on islands, shore, or ice floes.

Seals are great swimmers and divers. They cannot swim as fast as dolphins or whales, but they are even more graceful in the water. Some are able to stay underwater for more than thirty minutes.

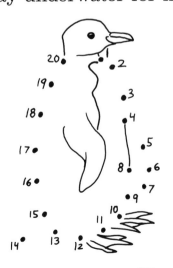

Leopard seals that live in Antarctica often eat penguins.

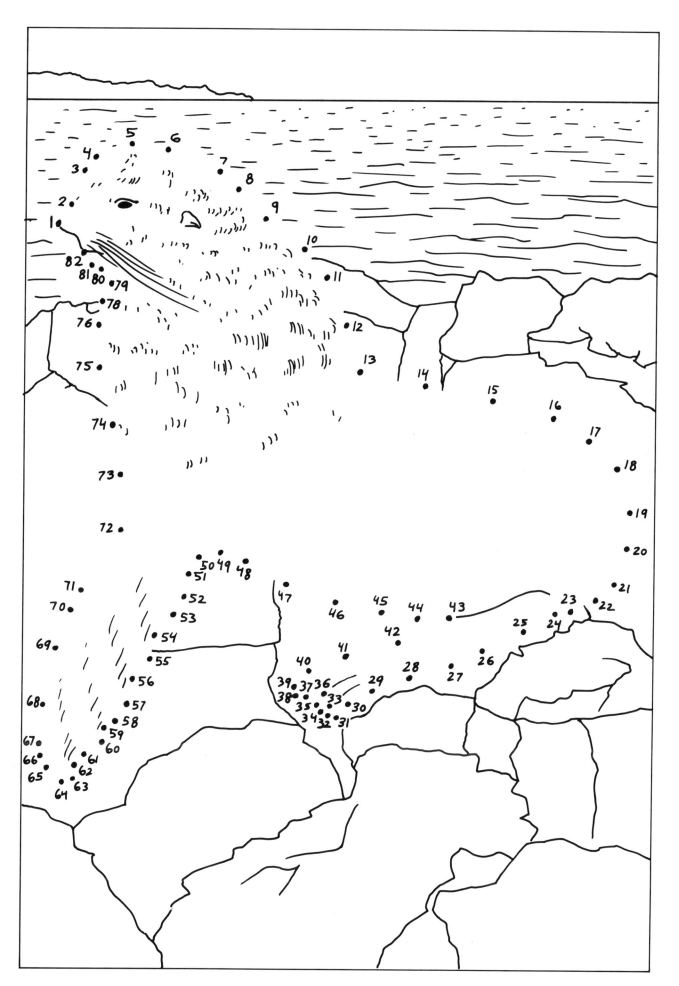

Sea Turtle

Size: Up to 7 feet (2.1m) long

Color: Shades of reddish brown to gray; or gray to green

What it eats: Mollusks, jellyfish, sea-grass, and algae

Where it lives: Usually in tropical seas around the world, but some travel far north.

Sea turtles have existed on earth for millions of years. They are one of the few reptiles that have adapted to life in the sea. They are cold-blooded, like other reptiles, and covered by a hard shell made up of scaly plates called "scutes."

Sea turtles never leave the water, except for the females, who come on land to lay eggs. When the baby turtles hatch, they head straight into the sea, and will stay there all their life, except for the females, who will return to the shore to lay eggs.

The female lays her eggs at night during the warmest time of the year. Then she covers them with sand and returns to the sea.

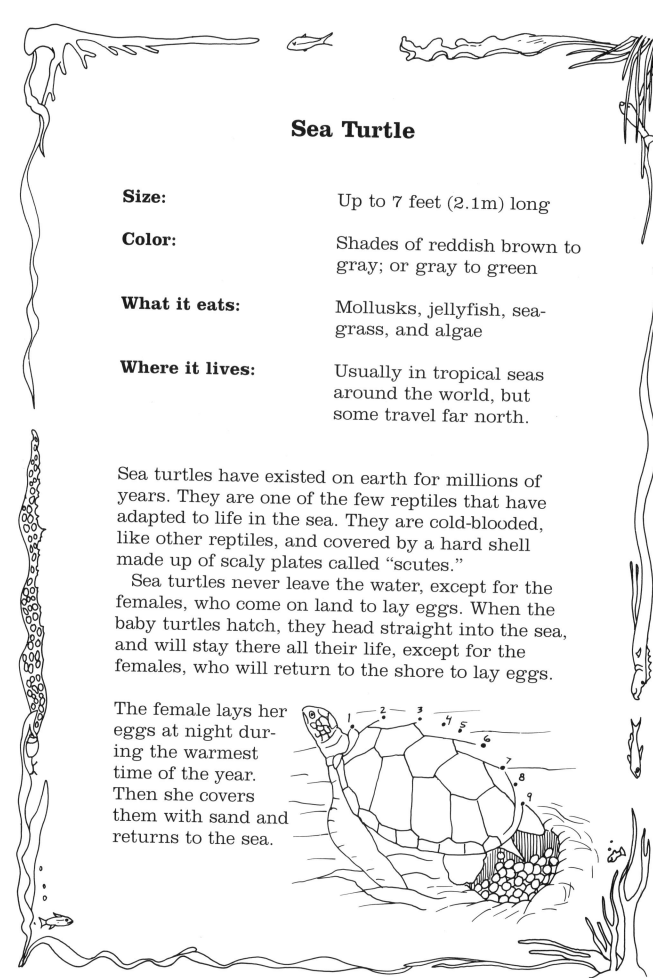

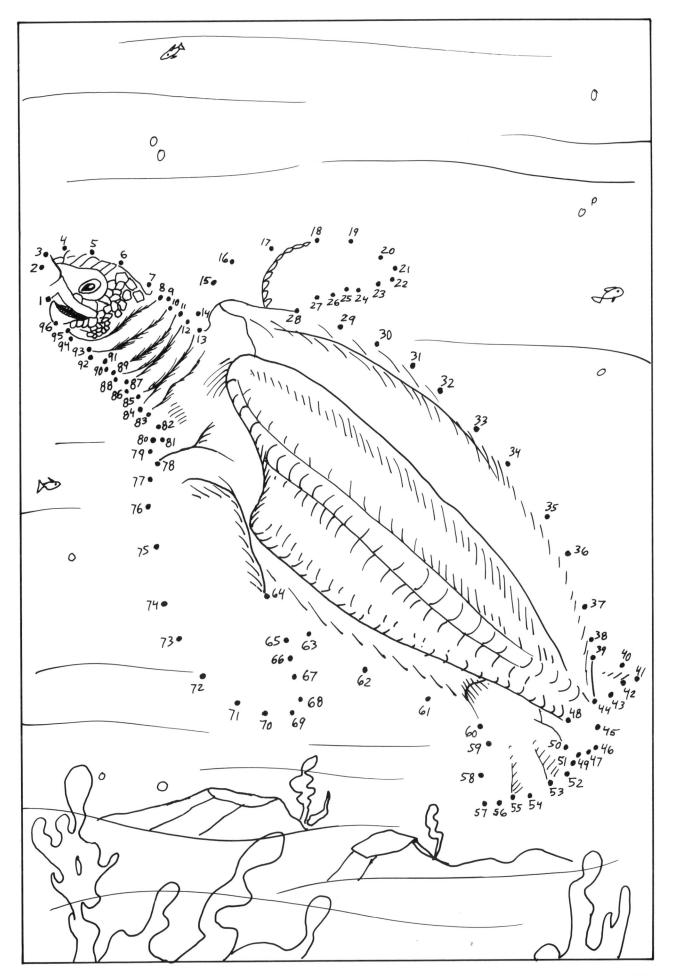

Squid

Size:

They range in size from less than ¾ inch to more than 65 feet (19.5m), including tentacles.

Color:

Red with spots, blue with spots, green with spots, yellow with spots, orange with spots. Like octopuses, they change colors to match the background and to match their moods.

What it eats:

Mostly fish, crustaceans, other squids

Where it lives:

Along the coasts and in the ocean

The squid has ten arms, eight like the octopus plus two long tentacles with suckers at the ends. A powerful swimmer, the squid moves by a kind of jet propulsion, sucking in water through openings in its neck and then shooting it out. It moves so powerfully it can even shoot itself out of the water!

Squids are an important food for many creatures, including fishes, sharks, dolphins, whales, and humans. The tuna (shown here) especially depends on the squid for food.

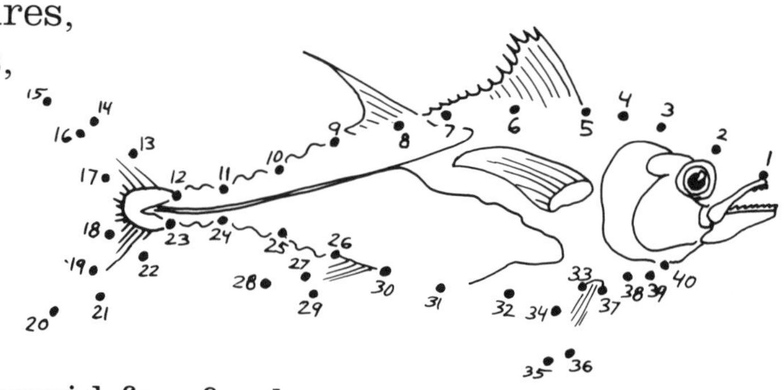

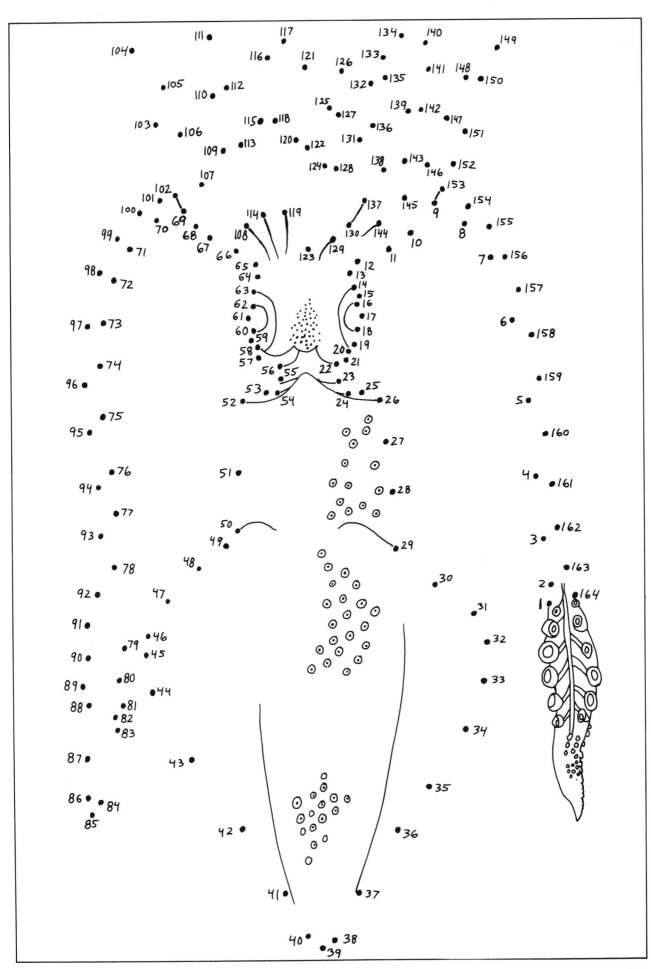

Starfish
(also called Sea Star)

Size:	Usually 6 to 12 inches (15 to 30cm) across, but some are less than half an inch, and others as much as 30 inches (75cm) across
Color:	Red, orange, yellow, and purple
What it eats:	Plankton and mollusks
Where it lives:	In all oceans

The starfish is one of the few creatures in the world that can lose one or more limbs and then grow new ones.

Each starfish has hundreds of tube feet that let it creep in any direction. If you watch closely, you may be able to see it move very slowly.

Not many fish can eat a starfish — or want to! But the sand tilefish does. It lives at the sea bottom, near a shelter it digs or builds out of rocks.

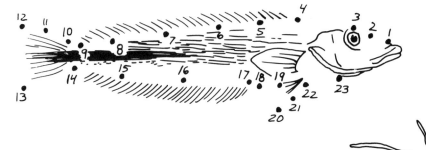

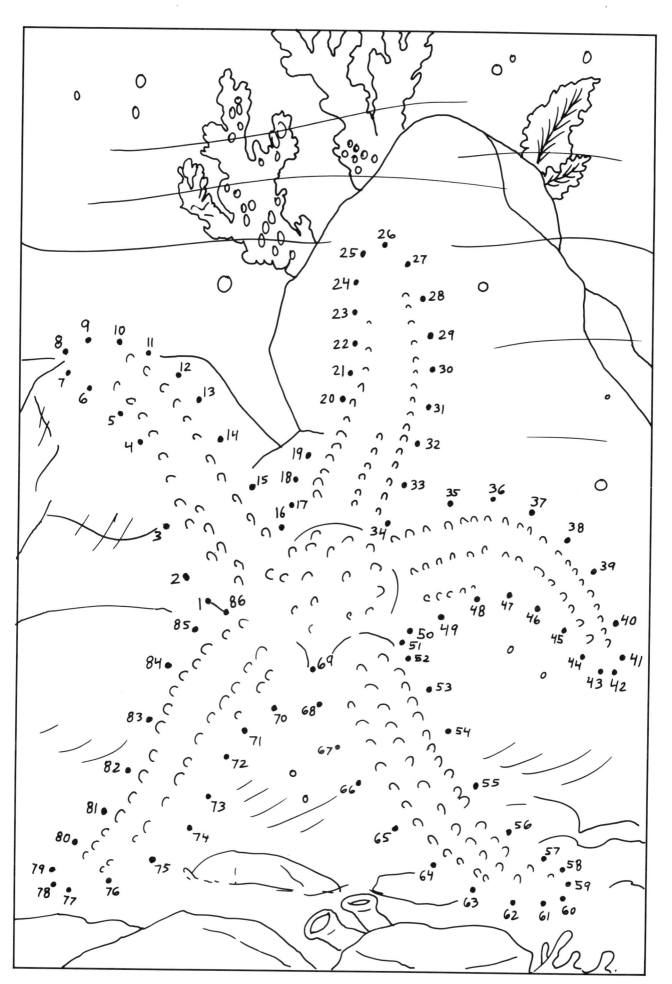

Swordfish

Size: Grows as large as 15 feet (4.5m) and can weigh as much as 1,000 pounds (450kg).

Color: Dark gray, black, purplish or bluish above and silvery below

What it eats: Smaller fish, squids, crustaceans

Where it lives: In warm and temperate oceans around the world

The swordfish is a long fish with no scales. It has a big fin on its back and a long sword coming out of its head which—unlike the Narwhal (page 34)—it uses to slash at its prey. Probably because it has the sword, the swordfish has no need for teeth. It is one of the very few fishes that has none.

   A difficult fish to catch, the swordfish can tire out the strongest fisherman, pulling for hours and hours on his line.

Not many creatures can catch a swordfish, but this Shortfin Mako Shark, as long as 12 feet (3.6m), is among the fast swimmers of the sea.

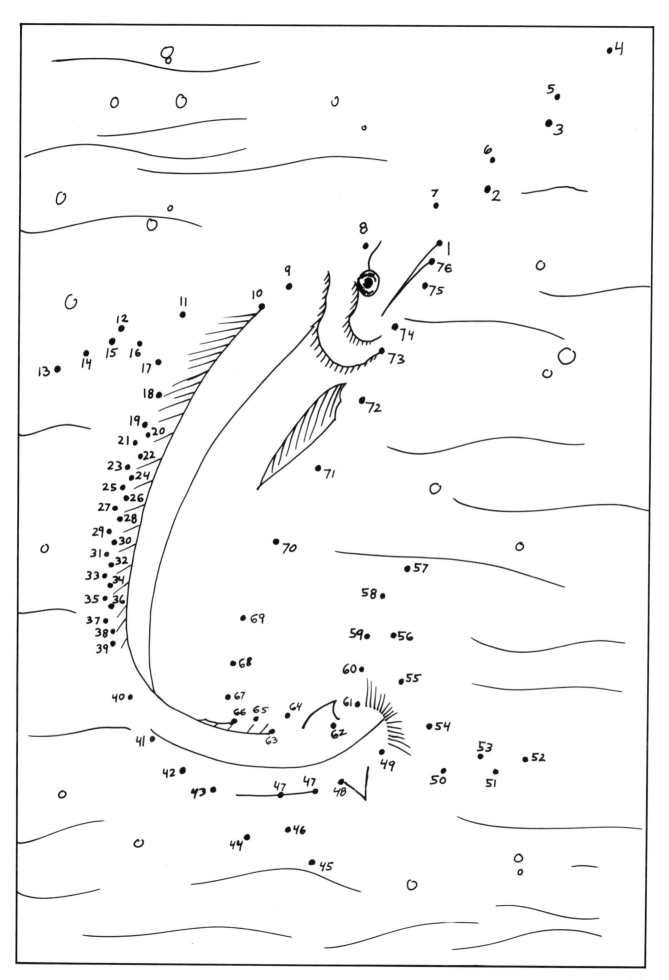

Viperfish

Size:	Up to 18 inches (45cm) long
Color:	Brown or deep red, sometimes with blue eyes
What it eats:	Fish
Where it lives:	Deep in the oceans, worldwide

In the deepest part of the ocean, there is no sunlight or green plants, and the temperature is almost freezing. How can you see anything at all? Viperfish have found a way! They actually have rows of lights on their underbellies that glow and attract their prey.

They also have extra big eyes, so they can see whatever light there is. They have extra large mouths, too, so that not a morsel of food is missed—and so that they can eat creatures their own size.

How do you think the viperfish got its name?

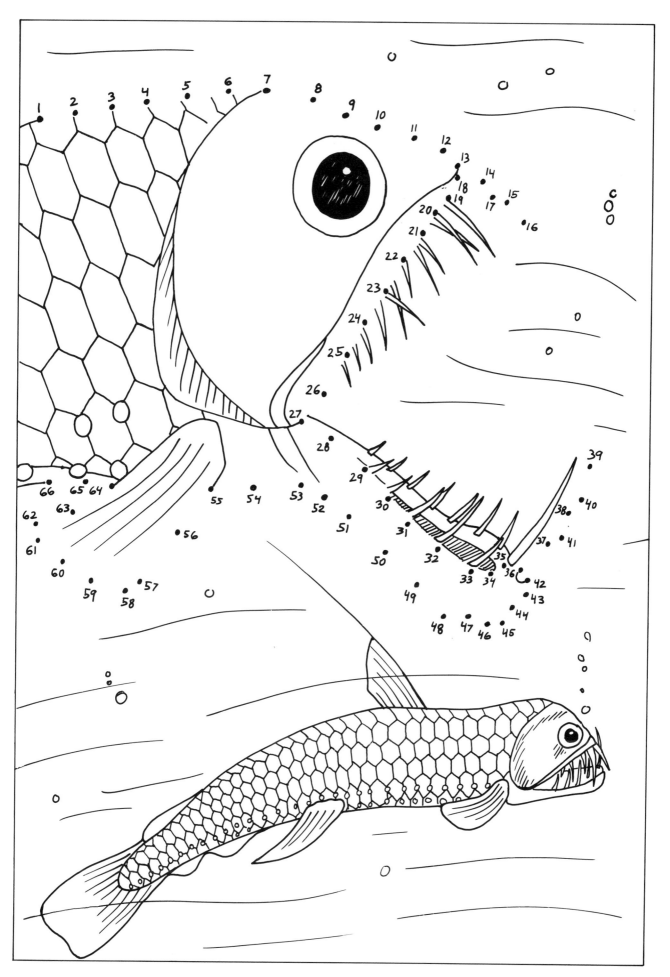

Wobbegong

Size: Up to 6 feet (1.8m) long

Color: Yellowish or brownish
                         with spots or stripes on its
                         back

What it eats: Fish and crustaceans

Where it lives: In coral reefs

The wobbegong is certainly an odd-looking shark.
It's known as the carpet shark because of the
fringes around its mouth and the carpet-like pat-
tern on its back. This lumpy fringed face makes it
look like the ocean floor, so the shark can easily
hide and surprise the small fish it wants to eat.

Can you see the
wobbegong hiding
here?

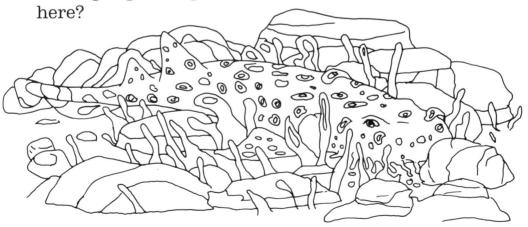

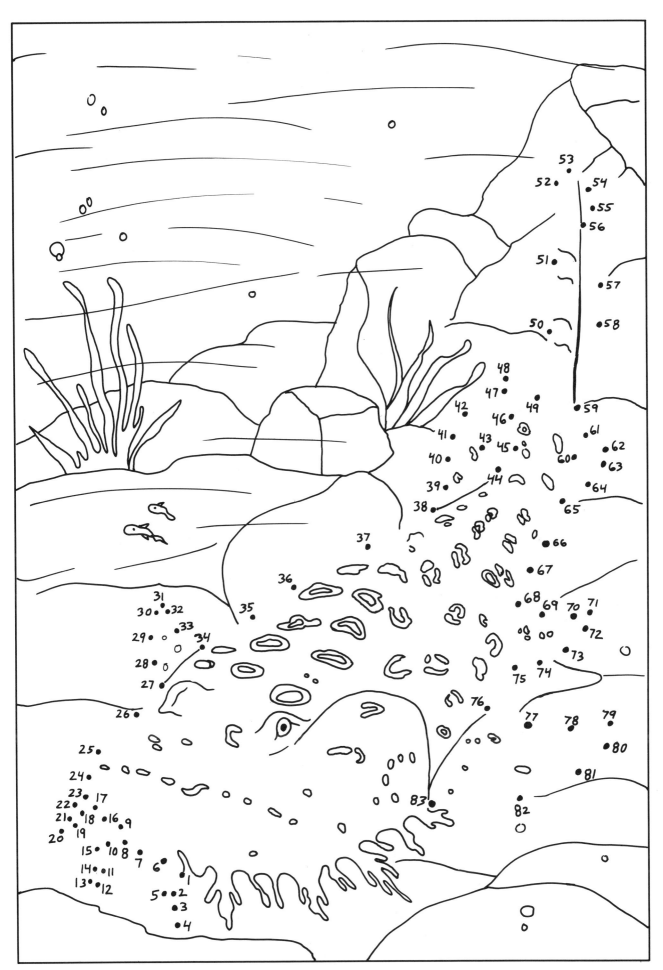

Index

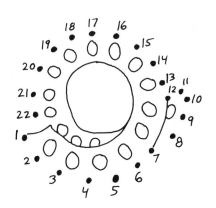